3

MIRACLES

and a

NEAR-DEATH
EXPERIENCE

Les & Dee
Jesus loves you!
Les J.B.

ISBN: 978-0-9905105-1-2

Published by Bright Lights Publishing

Editing and book design by Stacey Aaronson

First Edition
Printed in the USA

3
MIRACLES
and a
NEAR-DEATH
EXPERIENCE

by

LEE BREITKREUZ

BLP
BRIGHT LIGHTS PUBLISHING

CONTENTS

Everything happens for a reason.

—Romans 8:28

AS I APPROACH THE early winter of this short stint on earth, I find myself—as you may as well at times—looking back at certain extraordinary events that happened to me over the course of my lifetime. In fact, it wasn't until I turned 65 in 2011 that I realized it took many years, and one final miracle, to show me what was right in front of me all the time. Events in my life that at one time seemed to be confusing and isolated were actually quite connected, woven into God's tapestry using a common thread.

Of course, until you begin to view your life backwards, linking each event or experience to a prior one to see how one begat the next, it can be difficult to see the providence of the order of things. When we're living forward, we don't know what may come; when we view our life backward, we can see precisely why events happened the way they did. Many of us, however, don't tend to engage in this way of thinking until we've reached our more golden years.

I think most of us can agree that it's the "not knowing" part of life that's scary. It's a leap of faith to embrace that things happen for a reason, especially when those things are painful or don't seem to make sense. Traveling down my own life path, I struggled with many questions and frequently asked: Is there really a God? If so, is He putting me through the ringer to test me? Am I a bad person? If there is a God, is He punishing me through my misfortunes? Am I being penalized for my mistakes? If He loves me as much as the Bible says, why didn't He save me when I needed Him most?

It took three miracles to bless me with those answers, to give me insight into why He put me here at this time and place. But then, something else occurred, an event I never dreamed would happen to me. I wasn't sure at first how much I should share it, but every time I did, I was encouraged to share it more, that it was a gift I shouldn't keep to myself.

This is why I finally wrote my story.

It's important I tell you here that it doesn't matter if you're religious. It likewise doesn't matter if you have the same or different questions I had regarding spiritual issues. You may have a completely different view regarding God and religion than I do, and that's okay. I respect your convictions, no matter your beliefs. And if you happen to be agnostic or atheist, you should know that I'm not trying to convert anyone; I'm simply passing on a message, no more. I invite everyone to share my miraculous journey; all I ask is that you enter with an open mind, saving judgment for the end. If you glean anything else along the way that adds a spark to your heart light, or shifts your perspective toward loving yourself and others more, all the better.

1

IN THE BEGINNING

I CAME INTO THIS WORLD in 1946 in the small town of Hartford, Wisconsin, population 5,247, as the first of three boys born into dysfunctional chaos. My mother truly loved her children—Steve, Bill, and me —and being born approximately one year apart, she certainly had her hands full, not only because she had three babies to take care of, but because a darkness loomed over our family. And that darkness was my father.

From the age of three, my memories are extremely vivid, probably because many of my recollections are quite traumatic. My father, Leander Breitkreutz (rhymes with "Bright Lights"), had a disgraceful reputation. He was an alcoholic, well known in Hartford's taverns, and his late-night bar fights and antics on Main Street after the bars closed grew more frequent as time passed. Alcohol eventually ruined him, but not before destroying our family.

For most of my life, I kept secrets locked in a vault, the one we all have stowed deep inside our conscience. Many of us use it for hiding immoral, corrupt, or shameful memories we want no one to ever see or hear. I use mine for storing my deepest secrets and assorted emotions, the ones that are most difficult to reconcile as part of my existence. It is a vulnerable act to open that vault, but I've chosen to do so to illuminate the path my life took so that you can walk with me in the miraculous.

As a toddler and young boy, I spent many sleepless nights waiting in terror for Dad to come home. When he did, he would often physically abuse my mother, and sometimes me. One particular night, he engaged in hitting my mother with his fists in a one-sided shouting rant. I cowered in the shadows as pots and pans flew and glass shattered around me. Then, just when I thought the tirade was over, Dad swept over me and pinned my arms to my sides, pressed his face against mine, and shouted for me to stop crying. I couldn't. So he picked me up and took me to the kitchen sink, where he ran ice-cold water over my head and screamed at me to stop. When I still couldn't contain my tears, he threw me across the kitchen and I landed in the adjacent bedroom, wholly petrified.

I suddenly couldn't cry if I wanted to—and I did want to—because in that moment, a natural human emotion left my body. My young brain could not comprehend what had just happened, yet the evidence of the abuse was undeniable: both sides of my collarbone were broken.

I later learned the injuries had been classified as "falling out of my crib."

2

MOVING ON

B Y THE TIME I turned four in 1950, my mother was broken. Afraid, desperate, and penniless, she packed us up while Dad was at work and left our bare-bones attic apartment for refuge. We had lived in the lowest-rent district of Hartford—along the railroad tracks and next door to the Kraft cheese factory —and I remember the feeling of relief that my days of staring at the tracks and watching trains pass under the window were finally over.

The day we moved was sunny and cold. My mother carried Bill and a small suitcase; I held Steve's hand as we trekked the mile to Grandma Breitkreutz's house, the only place we had to go. Grandma was my dad's mother and was truly ashamed of his drinking and his lifetime of getting into trouble, often calling him "the black sheep of the family." Had it not been for her being on our side, we would have been forced to live on the street in constant fear of my father finding us.

That first night at Grandma's house was the most peaceful I had ever remembered. I can still feel the calm as though it were yesterday. I can also see with total clarity the vision of my mother coming down the stairs dressed in her Sunday best that next morning, looking beautiful and carrying her small suitcase. She was wearing a dress under a light winter coat and a fancy black hat with a little mesh veil over her red hair. When I looked at her closely, I realized she was trying not to cry and I knew something was wrong. That lovely vision immediately shifted to a rush of fear. Numbness entered my body as she called me over to the door; I sensed in my heart it would be the last time I would ever see her.

She gave me a long, mushy red lipstick kiss on the lips and cheek and a huge hug that I would have to remember for the rest of my life. Then she turned and walked out the door. The crying instinct that was damaged in me would not allow me to muster tears, but the anguish and devastation inside me was palpable. I needed a mother and mine just vanished forever.

Although Grandma was well aware of Dad's bad habits, she had no idea of his extreme behavior toward his wife and children. I was now the lone survivor of those horrors, forced to keep them locked in my subconscious. Steve, my brother eleven months my junior, had and still has a moderate mental handicap with no memory of those times; Bill was too young to have any recollection at all. I officially became the carrier of memories I believed I couldn't speak about, so I dutifully pushed them down and closed a door behind them.

DURING THE DAYS PRIOR to escaping our shabby apartment, my mother had made arrangements for my brothers and me to go to an orphanage in Milwaukee. My grandparents pleaded and argued with officials for months to keep us in their home, but they knew little about the laws concerning guardianship. As such, two officials came to the house once or twice a week and pounded on the door. Legally, they were required to remove us from Grandma's house, but she wasn't about to let that happen.

She instructed us to run upstairs and hide under the bed each time the men arrived. She would then go to the unopened door and shout in her broken English, "Youse go away and leave us alone once and for all! The boys are not here!" This worked for a time, but when the police finally accompanied the officials, Grandma was forced to let them in and escort us out. Tears streamed down my brothers' faces as Steve, Bill, and I were ripped from our grandparents' home and stuffed into the police car with our meager belongings as if we were criminals. We sat in silence the entire way to Milwaukee, having no idea what being placed in an orphanage would mean. Abandoned for the second time in our short lives, we felt completely alone and on our own, unsure if we would ever see our grandparents again.

THE INSTITUTION WAS PACKED with children of varying ages, and our caretakers were very strict about following rules, seeming resentful for having to care for us. Some, however, were quite kind, especially the ones in the nursery, but I nonetheless received many strong-armed escorts out upon being discovered searching for Bill and Steve. Lonely and concerned for my brothers, I often sneaked into the huge room with a high ceiling, dim lighting, and no windows, pungent with the scent of dirty diapers, where an ocean of wooden cribs zigzagged the floor with narrow, maze-like pathways for the caretakers. Almost every crib contained a crying infant or toddler, while those who grew accustomed to the noise slept through it.

Although the caretakers wanted no visitors in the way within the tight quarters, I would sometimes go unnoticed—since the cribs were taller than I was—as I snaked through the labyrinthian setup. With persistence, I would find my brothers. While Bill was a sleeper, Steve was almost always standing up and crying, wanting to escape with me. There wasn't much I could do to comfort him, and the helpless feeling consumed me.

I was placed in a room with older kids where, unlike the nursery, there was an odor of clean diapers drying somewhere nearby, the only somewhat pleasant smell in the building. Surrounded by stark, unwelcoming walls, rows of beds were lined up like obedient soldiers, and we were not allowed to talk after the lights went out at night. It didn't matter, though; the other kids were nonexistent to me. In fact, I don't recall making any significant friends. The entire setting was one I only remember as mundane, each day a boring clone of the one before as days turned into weeks, and weeks dragged into months.

After about a year, Grandma and Grandpa worked out the agreement to become our legal guardians. I was so grateful, I would have cried with joy if I could have. Though there were many reasons I wanted to leave that place, one was that I couldn't have eaten one more scoop of white rice. Every meal at the orphanage had a scoop, and I had to sit at the table until each grain was eaten. It was enough to make me white-rice averse for the rest of my life.

I RECALL NO GREATER joy and relief during that time than returning to our grandparents' house.

Grandma came to America from Germany in 1912 —from what she called "the Old Country"—and she met her soul mate in Grandpa shortly after he arrived here from Germany just a few years later. When Grandpa came to the U.S., he had no plan other than to survive. A teenager in a foreign land, he took up residence in Mayville, Wisconsin—and by residence, I mean camping in the woods and living off the land. He loved to tell me stories of how he subsisted on catching fish with gear constructed only of a long, bare tree branch, string, a safety pin for a hook, and earthworms for bait. He would wrap his catch in mud and throw it in the campfire to bake.

I'm not sure how my grandparents actually met, but they married soon after. Though economically they were borderline poor and sat at the bottom of middle class, they brought eight children into the world during the hardest of times in this country, just before the start of the Depression. The youngest died as an infant, but they raised the other seven as best they could, determined to make a good life for them in America. Although Grandpa worked hard, however, they remained relatively poor by choice.

After their children were grown and the opportunity to take my brothers and me into their home arose, they welcomed us without question. The term "empty nesters" meant nothing to them—they simply took care of their own because it was the right thing to do.

Grandpa always talked with a smile, proud of his accomplishments. Although short on education, he was long on mechanical abilities and personality, and he founded Hartford Radiator Service in Hartford, WI. It was a small business with a great reputation, and he took pride in his sons Norbert and Donald working for him as they came of age. He was an admirable male role model, for which I was grateful since he was the only one I really had.

Grandma, who was German through and through, held her rigid and opinionated heritage inside a short stature with a hard shell. Outsiders found her intimidating, but she was soft as butter on the inside. Over time, we became very close, and I sometimes wondered if I was the only one who knew how kindhearted she was under her rough exterior. She never said "I love you" or displayed outward affection, but I knew instinctively that she did indeed love us. Growing up with her hard, German way as an example, however, my inability to show emotions was compounded. I loved her dearly and thought of her as my second mother, but we never hugged or kissed or said we loved each other. The love she gave that resided inside of me, though, was enough to last a lifetime.

3

COST OF FREEDOM

A T THE AGE OF SIX, Grandma had me baptized into the Catholic Church. Hartford is located near the foothills of Holy Hill seven miles away—an enormous cathedral built on the highest hill in a heavily wooded area—and I remember going to Mass there once or twice a year with Grandpa and Grandma, who were not fond of all the steps and walking, yet deemed it an important family pilgrimage.

"Holy Hill" was named by Irish settlers, but the proper name is Holy Hill National Shrine of Mary, Help of Christians—a Roman Catholic shrine dedicated to the Blessed Virgin Mary. The centerpiece of the shrine is a minor basilica, and approximately 300,000 visitors come to the site each year. I remember a wall near Mary's shrine that displayed numerous crutches and canes left by healed visitors of long ago. It was my first feeling of connection with Mary, and it left an indelible impression on me.

I attended St. Killian Catholic School through eighth grade, then four years at Hartford Union High. Throughout these years, I was an excellent student and a fair athlete, but I was quiet, shy, and somewhat introverted. As abandoned children often are, I felt distant from my peers—as if I was on the outside looking in—and was frequently looked down upon because of my status in the pecking order. Not surprisingly, I was also awkward and unsuccessful with girls. I desperately wanted to be like those of my few friends who had "normal" lives with real parents. The truth was, I felt trapped and wanted to start my life over.

Despite my feeling out of place in most social circles, my aunt Millie and uncle Donald (who we affectionately call Shrimp—he's not a small person, but his childhood nickname happened to stick) were a great source of refuge, accepting me for who I was. Shrimp is Grandma's youngest son, and he and Millie allowed me to spend many high school nights on their couch, while their children, my cousins—Terry, Mary, Kathy, and even Sandy the dog—welcomed me with open arms as another sibling. My dreams of a loving and "normal" family were realized during the times I spent at Shrimp and Millie's house.

After graduating high school in 1964, I left Hartford. The nation and the world seemed to be in a holding pattern, still reeling in shock and disbelief seven months after President Kennedy's assassination. But I was intent on transforming my own emotions of sadness and fear from the tragedy into those of excitement—albeit with a new kind of fear.

With a meager scholarship and little over $900 saved from stocking grocery shelves, I felt wealthy and alive. It was the first time I was free and on my own—bounding into the spring season of my life—so although I continued to fear whatever unknown demons were lurking ahead of me, I was starting a fresh life and everything felt worth the risk.

Up to this point, life as a Catholic had been mediocre at best. I went through the motions of religion but did not see a real use for God as a savior. I constantly wondered where He was when I needed Him and decided that my new life would not include any God.

In lieu of college, I moved to Milwaukee and attended the Milwaukee Institute of Technology, working part-time to pay expenses. Back then, in the mid-60s, employers came to the school to interview graduating students and offered jobs on the spot to those most qualified. During one of these interviews, the Iowa Department of Transportation hired me as a surveyor, offering me a big-time salary of $4,000 per year, which was a good wage in 1966. I was on my way!

But after six months of traveling the county seat

towns of Iowa, enjoying my freedom and having the world by the tail, I was drafted into the Army. The Viet Nam era was upon us, and in my first months of basic and advanced infantry training at Fort Bliss, Texas, I found myself frustrated, angry, and scared to be re-immersed in yet another situation I could not control. In addition, I felt abandoned and alone for a third time in my mere twenty years on the planet. Worst of all, however, was that this time, my life was at stake. The entire situation, on the heels of Kennedy's death, cemented for me that there was no God. I had morphed into a real-life "Doubting Thomas," sucking up my feelings and locking them in the vault as usual, having no choice but to march forward within the confines of soldier-hood.

Despite my misgivings about being drafted, the Army turned me into an adult. I gained maturity and confidence that I hadn't anticipated, and about halfway through active duty, I began to feel proud to serve my country. Stationed in Germany, I spent my second year as a technician on Nike-Hercules guided missiles, each one the length of a semi-trailer. My unit was on standby to visit any trouble spot within range—via rocket-fueled, long-distance surface-to-surface missiles. If called, the conflict would have ended soon after, as our inventory included both large payload nuclear and conventional warheads. But thankfully, a year passed in Germany without incident, and in January of 1969, my tour ended and I came home with an honorable discharge. I was grateful that the fear I'd carried throughout my life had disappeared, but I still shouldered the burden of being alone. And it wasn't simply the loneliness itself that enveloped me, it was the bitterness and frustration that crept in, manifesting itself in my soul. My Catholic religion did nothing to help me shield myself from it; in fact, I began to see my religion as a "casualty of war."

4

THE FIRST MIRACLE

AFTER I WAS DISCHARGED, I returned to work, surveying for the Iowa Department of Transportation. Shortly after, I received a message from family that Grandma was in the hospital in Hartford and might not make it through the night. It was about 4 p.m. and without packing a thing, I left immediately from Pocahontas, Iowa, in my '55 De Soto and headed to Wisconsin.

It was the longest eight-hour-plus drive of my life. This was long before cell phones existed, so I had no way of receiving updates on Grandma's status. By the time I arrived at St. Joseph Hospital at 1 a.m., a nurse informed me that Grandma's heart was failing, cautioning me that she was unconscious and could pass at any time. I nodded numbly and found my way to her room along the dimly lit hallway and planted myself by her side.

My brothers and local family had visited earlier and gone home for the evening, so no one else was there. The room was dark except for the glow of the life-support machines beeping behind her headboard. Scanning the room, absorbing the near-quiet, I grasped the magnitude of the situation. The fact that she lay there dying increased my tremendous guilt for not coming home more often. I took her hands in mine.

"Grandma, can you open your eyes for me?" I whispered.

I sensed somehow that she was waiting for me to come home before leaving this world, that our closeness was keeping her alive until I could be with her. She slowly opened her eyes and stared into mine for a few seconds, then she closed them. Immediately after, the monitor cried that long, dreadful, steady tone as her heart stopped.

The nurse ran from her station, then paused in the doorway in respect of my presence. I quickly broke the German code and told Grandma that I loved her. I held her hands tighter and prayed a Hail Mary, the first time in years I had even considered prayer, save for the homemade ones I mumbled during the road trip to the hospital. This particular Hail Mary, however, was deep with emotion and sincerity.

Then something inexplicable happened.

As soon as I uttered "Amen," her monitor started beeping again. The nurse and I exchanged wide-eyed looks, then I turned back to Grandma to see if I was dreaming. I wasn't. I knew at that moment I had just witnessed a miracle. I didn't know at the time how long Grandma would live, but I swore I felt the presence of the Blessed Virgin Mary in the room, wanting me to enjoy my second mother for a longer time.

After a day or two of careful scrutiny by hospital specialists, Grandma—perfectly healthy—was discharged and sent home. Her doctor had no explanation for her sudden recovery.

IN SPITE OF BEING filled with overwhelming joy by Grandma's recuperation, an unfortunate reality hit me the day after the miracle: I couldn't share what had happened with my family. They would never believe a miracle had occurred; they would think the incident was purely coincidence. So, not wanting to risk their doubt and judgment—or their attempt to take this holy phenomenon away from me—I kept it to myself, privately rejoicing in finally holding a secret that wasn't painful. My spiritual capacity had instantly grown. I didn't believe I deserved God's grace, but I graciously accepted it. What's more, the miracle rekindled my Catholic faith. For the first time, I felt welcomed and accepted by God. I felt especially comforted by Mary, whom I recalled believing had a hand in healing the many disabled who traveled to Holy Hill for her help.

A spiritual bond developed between the Blessed Virgin and me. Mary became my third comforting mother, and the "Hail Mary" would forever be my first prayer of choice. It became undeniable to me that the power of prayer is enormous. Before Grandma's illness, I shamefully struggled with having a relationship with God. My spiritual life was a mess; I had conceded that there was no Higher Power. But after Mary joined me at Grandma's bedside, my eyes and heart opened as never before. I was forever changed, and my spiritual needs and desires were beginning to be fulfilled through newfound faith. As I felt myself expand and embrace my connection with the Divine, I realized its extraordinary power was accessible to all who seek it—and that it had been there all along, only I just wasn't awake enough to know it.

5

LIFE GOES ON

ONLY A COUPLE OF months after my Grandma miracle, I met my soul mate, Nancy. She was a game changer as I entered the next chapter of my life.

It started in June of 1969 when our survey crew was relocated to Winterset, Iowa. I had recently purchased a '67 Corvette Stingray, silver with a black racing stripe. My fellow crew member, Shep, happened to drive a '69 forest green Corvette, so we were a rare sight in this small county seat town. Shep had already met Chris, a girl he really wanted to date, and while Shep and I were on an evening cruise in my Vette, my friend spotted Chris with another girl. Both were in a phone booth (remember those?) and Shep elbowed me, insisting we stop and check out the girls for a possible double date. *This Corvette chick magnet really works!* I thought.

As we were introduced, I gasped upon seeing Nancy. I was twenty-two; she looked like "jail bait" to me, no older than sixteen. I remember that as Shep and Chris chatted, I noticed Nancy's bangs were fastened to her forehead with Scotch tape, which I thought was kind of funny. I wanted to talk to her, but we managed only a few forced words, after which we parted company and Shep and I drove off.

Over the next couple of weeks, Shep pleaded with me to ask Nancy for a date, and Chris badgered Nancy to accept if I did. We both finally relented, agreeing on the condition that it be a double date. Driving separately in our two-seat cars, Shep and I met the girls at the Red Hen Drive-In for pizza. It was a casual environment with plenty of people around, but I was nervous being out with such a young girl. My nerves were relieved, however, when Nancy told me she was home for the summer after her freshman year at the University of Northern Iowa. She was nineteen, not sixteen, which of course made a world of difference.

Prior to meeting Nancy, I had been relegated to dating only those who were desperate, but I could instantly tell that Nancy was different. She was someone I could take home to Grandma, which was a first. When she smiled, her eyes sparkled—and she smiled a lot. She was incredibly kind, and we had a fun time laughing, joking, and getting to know each other.

More dates followed with movies, eating out, picnics, and simply hanging out listening to music and sharing our thoughts. Our newfound friendship blossomed as we fell in love that summer.

A hidden benefit to our relationship was discovering Nancy's intimate connection to her parents—her "normal parents"—John and Lois Eve. I carefully observed how they interacted, and I felt the obvious love between them and with Nancy. Though my grandparents loved me, I couldn't help but long for the outward affection these people showed each other, secretly hoping they would show the same affection to me—and they did.

In August, Nancy had to return to UNI, and I asked to ride along and help move her back into the dorm. She agreed, but it was clear that she was anxious to get back to her college friends and life. Nancy shared later that her mom told her, "You'd better hang on to him because he would get you the moon if he could." I guess my feelings for her were pretty transparent to her mom; however, Nancy wasn't totally convinced. She felt the need to test us, to see if we loved each other enough. She allowed me to come visit on weekends, which I did as often as possible, and by Thanksgiving it was clear to both of us that we were soul mates made in heaven.

Nancy's parents knew we were serious, and they supported our relationship completely, but they did ask for one thing: that Nancy finish college before getting married. During that two-and-a-half-year waiting period —which felt more like decades—Nancy did something bold: she started attending Mass and taking classes to convert to Catholicism. She had been raised a Methodist, and her mother was very active in the church and strong in her faith, so Nancy wasn't sure how she would take the decision. When Nancy talked to her mother about converting, however, she responded with incredible openness. "Worship God together," she said, "no matter what church." It was a welcomed gift to both of us, and my grandparents were of course delighted.

As I committed my life to Nancy, I wanted more than a traveling job for the rest of our life together, so I gave up my surveyor's career, signed up for the GI Bill —the military benefit for college- -and decided to pursue landscape architecture at Iowa State University. I chose this field because I was drawn to the outdoors and loved beautiful landscapes, and with a fervent commitment to my educational goal, I enrolled at ISU in the fall of 1970 and completed a five-year program in four. On June 3, 1972, exactly one week after Nancy's UNI graduation, we were married. We didn't have a penny to our names, but we were happy clams and life was good.

One month later, Nancy accepted a job with the Ankeny school system as an elementary teacher. By August—with the help of Nancy's uncle Willard, president of a Winterset bank—we were able to acquire a $5,000 loan to purchase a mobile home in Ankeny, a place we quickly came to love. We joined Our Lady's Immaculate Heart Catholic Church, and Ankeny has remained our hometown ever since.

NANCY'S PARENTS TRUSTED OUR reckless decision to commence our married life with nothing in the bank, perhaps because they saw something in our relationship that transcended money. With a strong early impression that deepened during Nancy's final year of college, I won John's and Lois Eve's hearts—and they won mine. I also forged wonderful relationships with her brothers, Larry and Paul, who had approved of my "stealing away" their sister. I spent many weekends at their rural Winterset home enjoying their camaraderie and home cooking, discovering what real parents were like. Because of her commitments at school, Nancy wasn't always present, but those times alone with her parents were some of the fondest of my life.

I adored Nancy's mom. We had a connection I cannot explain. She had a special twinkle—the one Nancy so beautifully inherited—in her large brown eyes that greeted me every time I saw her, and she truly grew to love me like a son. In fact, Lois Eve looked so forward to my visiting on the weekends that at times it almost seemed as if she preferred me over Nancy. Although I often didn't believe I had much more to share than my parents being divorced and being raised by my grandparents, we would talk long into the night about any number of topics. Those talks meant the world to me; she was the first person I felt I could really open up to without judgment and share my opinions on anything. As much as I loved my grandmother, Lois Eve truly became the mother I never had.

One of her favorite things to do with me was go for rides around town on my motorcycle. She loved the wind in her hair, the feeling of youth and freedom that an open-air ride can give a person, and after awhile I conceded to teaching her how to drive. We quickly learned, however, that it was best for me to remain the driver. On the day she took the front seat for the first time in her large backyard, she panicked and ran the bike up the trunk of a mature white pine, falling off on the way up. As she thudded to the ground, I rushed to her side, afraid of what injuries she might have sustained. But as she lay there, with laughter and tears pouring out simultaneously, she assured me no serious harm was done. After I helped her up and confirmed she hadn't broken anything, she gratefully went back to being a passenger.

While Lois Eve was endlessly enthusiastic and adventurous, Nancy's father was a quiet, pipe-smoking, keenly observant man of few words. He, too, possessed a twinkle in his eye, but his said, "You had better be the right one for my girl. So far I don't see much." But time broke the ice, especially after we discovered we had something in common: pheasant hunting. Only our first experience together wasn't quite what either one of us bargained for.

It was the winter of 1970, and we were on John's friend's farm, parked near the barn. As we began walking, a rabbit ran out from under a nearby barbed-wire fence. My immediate thoughts were, *Does John like to eat rabbit? Will he be upset if I don't shoot?*

Intent on impressing him but unsure of whether or not to shoot, I hesitated, then abruptly fired my gun and missed. While I tried to hide my embarrassment as the grateful rabbit sped away, an epic roar rose up from the side of the barn, outside my line of sight. Within seconds, a scared herd of about twenty cattle formed a stampede, running at amazing speed down the steep hill through a large plowed and frozen field, downing the fence we had just crossed. I stood in shock as they flushed out about 50 pheasants a half mile away in a slew, destroying our hunting opportunity. No cattle were harmed, but we spent the entire afternoon rounding them up and mending fences.

Needless to say, we did not bond as men do after a great day in the outdoors; in fact, John remained quiet throughout the weekend until he finally broke into a smile at the end of our last day, giving me an unspoken sign that all was forgiven—and that perhaps he liked me more than I realized.

FOR FIVE YEARS, we continued to grow as a "normal family." I received my Bachelor of Science degree in landscape architecture at ISU in May of 1974 and immediately started my landscape business. Then, in the midst of our joy, a bomb was dropped on us: Lois Eve was diagnosed with terminal breast cancer. Naturally, we were devastated. By the time they discovered it, the disease had already spread to her liver; doctors called it aggressive and gave her only six weeks to live, suggesting she try the then-experimental treatment of chemotherapy. Having no other known alternative, she agreed as we all stood by her, unclear of what to expect.

Although it was a rough time for her, the chemo actually bought her another three years, which all of us embraced as a remarkable gift. Yes, she had pain and bad days, but she also had a great deal more time with us, as well as time to prepare for what was to come. I prayed my Hail Mary prayer and many others throughout Lois Eve's illness, but though she survived much longer than we anticipated, there was no miraculous healing for her. I refused to let spiritual doubt creep back into my mind, however. I maintained faith that a cure was perhaps in our future, that maybe I simply needed to pray harder—so I did.

As grateful as we were to have Lois Eve still with us, she could no longer live a carefree life, which proved to be pure heartbreak for John. Not only did he suffer seeing her decline, but he had always been so dependent on her that he couldn't function. It was during this time that he realized how much she truly meant to him, and he was able to tell her how he felt. Knowing Lois Eve so well, Nancy and I knew how touched she would be to hear those words from her husband, and we couldn't help but wonder if perhaps that was one reason she was given the extra years.

IN THE SUMMER OF 1977, our new dream home was under construction on beautiful wooded acreage in rural Ankeny that I had chosen for us. Our happiness was tainted, however, by the failing health of Lois Eve. When she and John came to visit our new home site, she was sporting a wig to cover her chemo baldness, and walking for her had become difficult. The house was framed, sided, and had windows, but it lacked interior finish and steps to the front door, so with the assistance of John and me, Lois Eve conquered the temporary wooden ramp. I could see the approval in her eyes as she smiled and peered inside, giving us her blessing without saying a word. It was at this moment that I realized she would never see the finished product.

We all marched forward into the unknown like good soldiers, but we knew the end was near. Larry and Paul, who lived nearby in Winterset, were always there to give support, and it wasn't long before Lois Eve was admitted to a Des Moines hospital.

Although none of us wanted to think of any visit as our last, I recall realizing the day that would be mine. Nancy was sitting on the bed and I was at the foot. Lois Eve was too weak to talk and medications were protecting her from most of the pain. The yellow tint of her skin was more prolific than the previous visit, and Nancy was crying and holding her hand. Lois Eve stared at me for a long while with her large brown eyes, which had lost their characteristic twinkle, seeming to ask, "Is it time?" My sad, watery eyes replied, "It's time. You have suffered enough."

Despite the heroic measures taken to save her, Lois Eve passed away at the early age of 61, in September of 1977. Besides my sadness for Nancy and her father, I was equally shattered myself. Another "mom" had left me. Only this time, something unexpected happened: my carefully guarded emotions that I normally filed away came flooding out, allowing me to mourn her loss. It was incredibly freeing to give myself permission to grieve, and Nancy lovingly embraced what she knew was an extremely vulnerable state for me. Even though it was difficult, it was a meaningful turning point in our relationship. What made it even more bittersweet is that only one month after her mother died, Nancy discovered she was pregnant.

EIGHT MONTHS LATER, in 1978, Matthew Lee was born. On a scale of one to ten, our happiness meter soared toward infinity. Although John, Nancy, and I were brokenhearted that Lois Eve would never get to hold her grandchild, we allowed our joy as new parents to overshadow our sadness in missing her, believing in our hearts that's what Nancy's mom would have wanted. And the arrival of Matthew brought another blessing: John's deep-seeded bitterness, self-deprivation, and loneliness transformed into pride and happiness upon becoming a grandfather, as he sincerely loved and cared for his infant grandson.

Only one year later, we received another difficult blow, losing another dear family member when my grandfather passed away. Proud to have raised ten children and sustained a well-loved business for decades, he died a rich and content man, peacefully dozing off in a lawn chair overlooking his vegetable garden. Our loss was heaven's gain.

In 1982, our daughter and princess Amy Beth came along, and our hearts grew full again. Now blessed with two healthy, beautiful children, it seemed that life could not get any better. We were living the American dream, but it wasn't without its ups and downs—the summer of my life would prove to be a roller coaster ride of elevated happiness ... and devastating sadness.

IN THE FALL OF 1984, Nancy's dad developed a speech problem, slurring his words and drooling without control. Through the process of elimination, doctors at the Veterans Administration Hospital and the University of Iowa Hospital in Iowa City diagnosed his disorder as Amyotrophic Lateral Sclerosis (ALS), otherwise known as Lou Gehrig's Disease. A progressive neurodegenerative disease that affects nerve cells in the brain and the spinal cord, early symptoms of ALS often include increased muscle weakness—especially involving the arms and legs—as well as a decline in speech, swallowing, or breathing. With voluntary muscle action progressively affected, patients in the later stages of the disease often become completely paralyzed.

Less than two years after his diagnosis, John died in June of 1986 at the age of 73. We intensely mourned his loss, and losing both of Nancy's parents at such an early age gave Nancy and me an undeniable sense of abandonment. Though in many ways her father's death was a merciful one, we were brokenhearted that Matt and Amy would no longer have a loving grandparent nearby, which is so important in a child's life. Although my father was still alive, he was hardly a loving grandparent, not to mention a child's role model. In fact, as our children grew up, I never wanted them to come into contact with my father, who still resided somewhere in the Hartford area. Thankfully, we endured only a few awkward visits when Dad popped in unannounced at Grandma Breitkreutz's house, setting me on edge as I watched him attempt to be grand-fatherly.

Despite the fact that Grandma was becoming frail, she always looked forward to seeing her great-grandchildren, and we made as many trips as possible to Wisconsin to see her, Bill, and Steve. Perhaps I believed when Grandma's time came, it would be like before, with enough time to travel to be by her side. So when we received a phone call one day in 1990 from Steve that Grandma had passed away quietly in the night, all four of us were devastated. Though I was particularly sad that the children had no more grandparents to speak of, I was also markedly affected that a chapter in my life had undeniably closed, my last "mother" finally leaving me. Despite those feelings of loss, however, I was also consumed with gratitude that after surviving her "incurable" condition nearly twenty years before—seemingly with the aid of my simple prayer—Grandma had truly proven to be a miracle ... blessing us with many more cherished memories before trading her earthly body for her eternal heavenly one.

6

FORGIVENESS

OVER THE YEARS, I learned more from Grandma and other relatives about Dad's history after my mother left him. My parents divorced but Dad continued his drinking, this time with another woman. Her name was Lois, and they created a baby out of wedlock who was removed from their home after police discovered the baby abandoned. As a result, my dad and future stepmother were arrested and sent to prison.

When Dad and Lois completed their prison time, they married and had three more children. My half-sister, Betty, and half-brothers, Richard and Ron, were very close to Dad. He apparently had an epiphany and strove to leave his vile ways behind him, determined to make this new family more close-knit and harmonious.

When I saw him for the first time in many years, it was clear that his demeanor had changed. He drank less and spent more quality time with his other family. Though it was hard to see him be a loving father toward his new children, I found it impossible to harbor any animosity toward them. Richard was especially likable and friendly, and I knew it would be wrong to try to taint my new siblings' version of their father with mine. Despite my noble efforts to be "above it all," though, I admit the awkward situation was hard to swallow. Not only would my conscience not allow me to trust his "magical transformation," but it was also a bit too close to home—Dad's new life unfolded in front of my brothers and me in the same small town in which our grandparents raised us.

Steve and Bill never left Hartford. Grandma wanted Steve to inherit the house, knowing he would not easily adapt to another environment. So to avoid an avalanche of ill feelings and questions from certain relatives, Grandma and her attorney devised a legal "sale" of the house to Steve long before her death. In the end, Grandma's decision was viciously attacked—she did have six other living children besides us—but ultimately not contested. As a result, Bill and Steve still live in our childhood home where good memories were nurtured and where we felt safe. Bill has stayed by Steve's side, as

he needs a degree of assistance, providing transportation and brotherly companionship. It warms my
heart to see the sibling devotion between them, and I
can't help but believe God had a finger in this plan too.

As Dad reached his later years, he made several
feeble and counterfeit attempts at becoming "friends"
with Steve and Bill, visiting for a few hours at a time,
two to three times a week. With Dad's tremendous gift
of pointless gab—most of his stories were repeated
whoppers—there was no end to his rambling, and my
brothers' gentle and accepting nature made it difficult
to tell him it was time to leave.

After four or five years of this habitual visitation
that my brothers felt somehow obligated to support,
Dad passed away in 2008, at the age of 84. Bill called
and told me the news only a few days before the
funeral; he had learned of Dad's death by reading it in
the obituaries. My half-sister Betty took charge of
arrangements but didn't notify Steve, Bill, or me
directly. I understood why she didn't because she must
have felt we were outsiders in their family. It would have
been easy, therefore, for us to let the funeral slide by
like any other day of the week, but we felt we had some
awkward duty to be there.

Steve and Bill wanted to pay their final respects, and
out of moral support for my brothers—and pure
curiosity for me—Nancy and I decided to go. We drove
400 miles from Ankeny to Hartford, all the while

wondering if I would experience any kind of emotion besides the numbness, disgust, and contempt that had been locked deep in the vault nearly all of my life. Shrimp and Millie were the only people I had shared some of these feelings with; the rest of my friends and family had no idea what I had endured.

As I mingled with long-lost relatives and military men in uniform in the gathering space of the church, I noticed military displays in Dad's honor. I spotted his Purple Heart and other medals earned in WWII in a glass case, medals tarnished and dusty from years of neglect. It was strange to think of Dad as an American WWII hero. What kind of hero would fight for his country and then come home to marry, have kids, and harm his loved ones?

I began to reflect on Dad's military experience, standing there amidst the crowd, their low murmuring fading out and away as if a protective dome had been placed over me. Dad had been shot in the knee but refused to allow doctors to amputate his leg. Rather than wear an artificial limb, he opted to live in pain for years. As a veteran myself, this decision struck me hard, making we wonder if I would have done the same. Then I began to imagine the loneliness, heartache, and pain he must have felt, scared and alone in a foreign country. France was not good to him. Violence and death was everywhere.

My mind started to swirl with questions I'd never considered before. *Had Dad come home from the war with bottled-up emotions and anger, along with pain, that he didn't have the capacity to deal with? Did he suffer from post-traumatic stress disorder?* I, of course, will never know, and it was not for me to judge. But what happened in that pocket of reflection was that I discovered something good about him, about something he had done with his life, and I suddenly saw him differently. I turned then and walked down the main aisle to the front of the church. Alone there, I peered into the casket and saw an old man with thin gray hair. I said a prayer and then forgave him for destroying our family. I felt my heart open in that moment, and I sincerely hoped he found peace.

As I turned away from the casket, I noticed a female stranger sitting in the front row with my half-siblings and wondered who she was. She seemed to be part of the family, but I'd never seen her before. Curious, I made my way to the back of the church where Steve, Bill, and Nancy were sitting. We hadn't been invited, and we wanted to remain a bit in the periphery so as not to upset anyone. But afterward, Betty approached me and asked if I would accept Dad's military flag during the closing ceremony at the cemetery. I humbly agreed.

In the midst of the hushed conversation that followed the ceremony, I discovered that the stranger in the first row—now a grown woman—was the baby Dad and Lois had abandoned all those years ago. She had been adopted, and after extensive research on her part, she found Dad and Lois a few years prior to Dad's death. It was an awkward revelation to discover I had another sibling, but when we were introduced, something inside of us clicked and we quickly bonded as brother and sister.

FORGIVENESS IS NOT SUPPOSED to be easy. We sometimes have pain that we can't forget, and it's hard to let that go. But forgiveness is not about forgetting; it's about giving up the hope that the past can be any different. When I forgave my father, I offered him a powerful dose of mercy—and a gift of mercy to myself as well. I had no tears to shed for him, but what I gave was far more important.

To this day his American flag, folded in the triangle as presented to me, is stored in a place of prominence in my home—with the bullet casings from his salute tucked inside the fold. And my new sister, Chris, and I ... we've continued to get to know each other better, staying in touch since that day, proving that gifts can come in a myriad of unexpected ways.

7

THE SECOND MIRACLE

SHORTLY AFTER MY RETURN to Ankeny from the funeral, I reluctantly agreed to attend a men's retreat—Christian Experience Weekend (CEW) —hosted by my home parish, Our Lady's Immaculate Heart Church. Friends had been hounding me to attend this annual event for the past six years, but they would never disclose what happens during the weekend. Each time they prodded me to go, I politely declined with some lame excuse. I did not want to spend three of my precious days off at some secretive "camp." More than that, I was repulsed by the thought of being associated with a group of men like those I witnessed each year after a CEW. Grown men would bear-hug in public, and to make it more obnoxious, they would loudly slap each other's backs while doing so. I found this beyond arresting, but I relented that year simply to put an end to the nagging. No matter what, though, I was resolute that I was not going to hug anyone.

Shortly into the weekend, I could feel the Holy Spirit within me. To my surprise, I felt compelled to open my vault and share my deepest secrets with strangers. As if enveloped in a sudden cocoon of safety, I spewed my childhood story, confessed my hatreds, lamented my missing emotions, and expressed my desire to be loved. It was a healing moment, a God-moment, an epiphany. I received an enormous gift that weekend, allowing the Holy Spirit to move through me and unlock that burdened part of my soul. Buried emotions came alive; I cried (in private). Awkward hugging and loud patting of backs ensued, and I no longer found it wholly offensive.

While the weekend was powerful and ignited an evolution in me, I must admit it was—and remains—difficult to be openly affectionate when I wasn't raised that way. Being demonstrative simply feels a bit unnatural, especially with people I barely know, which I've learned is not uncommon for children who were brought up without much physical affection. For the record, I've become a hugger when one is requested, but it is still very uncomfortable for me, especially with males; in fact, I never initiate a man-hug. I don't mind giving hugs to family and close friends, but I still prefer a good, firm handshake.

IN JANUARY, 2011, I was asked to be the director of Christian Experience Weekend. I was at once honored and terrified, believing I was underqualified to take on such a role, but I accepted nonetheless. Preparation began six months prior to the event, and confident in my business background, I easily led meetings, recruited, and organized sixty to eighty team members. Scheduling, emailing, and calling people was a non-issue; the part I feared was being in a closed room with men who would most likely express life-altering concerns and questions that I might feel unqualified to respond to appropriately. Despite my trepidation, however, up until just hours before the weekend started, I convinced myself I could handle it on my own. I was wrong.

It was 1 p.m. on Friday, six hours before most of the guests would be arriving, and my fears began to take over. Tension magnified tenfold, and I had the sinking feeling it was too late to ask for help. In last-minute desperation, I slipped into St. Michael's private prayer chapel down the hall from the event.

The chapel was a new wing off the daily Mass chapel, octagon in shape with beautiful stained glass windows on all sides that cast colored light over those inside. The single open entry invited parishioners into the sacred space, with a vaulted wood ceiling and a glass cupola. Chairs and kneelers lined the perimeter while the center of the room held the wooden tabernacle—an ornate, locked, box-like vessel placed on a pedestal for the exclusive reservation of the consecrated Eucharist. We Catholics believe a person in the presence of the Eucharist (communion host) is in the direct presence of God.

My friend Daryl was the only person in the room. The chapel was restricted to silent prayer, but since there were no other visitors, we broke the silence rule. I asked him to pray a rosary with me, and together we prayed the Joyful Mysteries. This gave me temporary calm; however, after Daryl left, my anxiety escalated again. Out of nowhere, I said an emotional spontaneous prayer that went something like this:

Holy Father, I hate to bother you with such a trivial request. You know I'm very concerned about this weekend. I don't want to ruin it for the participants with my feeble actions. Please be with me and give me the courage to lead with confidence.

With a deep breath of relief for having expressed my needs, but having no expectations, I headed toward the door for my next pre-event meeting down the hall, stopping first to genuflect. When I turned my back to the tabernacle and walked across the threshold of the entry, I abruptly felt a tremendous weight pressing down on my shoulders as if someone was pushing me toward the floor. Rather than being afraid of the force, however, I immediately sensed that it was the goodness and grace of God pouring into me. My body tingled from my shoulders to my feet, and my knees buckled as I briefly lost balance, but when I straightened up, I felt incredible calm and peace come over me, suddenly feeling confident with no worries.

During the next meeting, I was physically present but spiritually elsewhere, overwhelmed with what had happened to me. I couldn't help but see it as yet another miracle occurring in my life. With the weekend upon me, I was curious how events would play out.

ONE OF THE MANY purposes of the CEW is to strengthen and enrich the attendees' relationship with God. It is believed that a special time and private place, away from the busy routine of daily living, is where a true Christian community can develop in a variety of ways. For example, the participants eat and sleep within the confines of the retreat to shut out all distractions. They are likewise asked to turn off cell phones and electronic communications for the weekend. Clocks are even removed from the walls and watches are put away so that the concept of time is not an issue. Although not a retreat consisting of silence and meditation, there is time for that if the participant feels the need. Ultimately, it is a shared Christian experience that grew out of the realization that the Christian life has to be experienced before it can be properly appreciated.

Because there is hope that a participant's experience will profoundly affect him spiritually, a moderate form of secrecy is promoted so that the participants will go forth and invite others to join the next retreat. By not divulging details about the weekend, attendees are able to entice future participants to come see why there is so much joy within that individual.

Prior to CEW, I had virtually no experience with public speaking. My shy and introverted personality had been a roadblock, so while I was confident when giving a presentation of a landscape design to a client, that was usually one-on-one, or at most, in small groups.

As the master of ceremonies for CEW, however, my job was not only to make a large group of participants feel at home, but also to calm their fears. As you may imagine, many people attend out of curiosity yet are afraid it may not be for them, while others come with a chip on their shoulder because they're upset with God and the church and need to vent, while still others are shamed into coming by peers or spouses and have no real desire to be there.

Instead of feeling the panic I would normally experience, I somehow felt power, encouraging participants to become engaged. I lead small group conversations that developed new friendships and a sense of community. Intense spiritual feelings evolved from sharing fears, problems, joys, and everything in between. Despite my lifelong comfort with introversion, I miraculously transformed into a true leader, receiving courage from God to elaborate on otherwise uncomfortable topics and embracing God-moments when they were given to me, believing I was meeting the men's expectations of being a mentor.

For one example, a participant shared with me his extreme anger over being pitied. He had a physical disability, and according to him, most people talked to him as if he had a mental handicap. I happened to know that he was extremely intelligent, and I understood his frustration over consistently being treated in this manner. As I listened without judgment, he then began to complain at length about his physical appearance. Though I normally would have tried to make him feel better by deflecting his comments, I instinctively remained silent. After a bit, the man regained composure and retreated from his rant with an apology. At that point, I said, "Let me tell you something. I look at my body as a vessel. It's imperfect just as everyone is imperfect. I'm not close to perfect by any means, and this body will die someday and become just an empty vessel. Whatever vessel we have, it is in the likeness of God. I believe our challenge is to use what we have to serve and honor Him. It's about what we do with what we have." I knew the words didn't come from me, but rather from God *through* me, and they seemed to create a shift in this man's thinking. Our conversation then turned to heartfelt prayer.

The entire weekend was filled with more experiences like this one, with men being spiritually moved in my presence from God using me as a conduit of inspiration and understanding. To witness a spiritual transformation of forty strangers before my eyes was more than I could have asked for, and needless to say, I witnessed a myriad of guests leave with a closer connection to God, as did I.

AS I'VE SHARED, the Hail Mary is still my chosen structured prayer, but I've also learned that spontaneous prayer—which comes from the heart—is incredibly powerful. When we talk to God directly, not confined by specific words or cadences, we're able to be our authentic selves, and I believe God understands and appreciates our genuine expression of emotions, no matter what they may be. I, myself, pray this way often, in the privacy of a secluded place with little or no outside noise, and I eliminate distractions by closing my eyes. At first, my intimate conversation with God feels one-sided. Then I pause and listen. Many of us find that silence and listening are virtues that take a great deal of practice and patience—I know I do—and I try diligently to not get frustrated waiting for instant results. But what I've found is that the longer I listen in silence, the greater my experience. Ultimately, these spontaneous, from-the-heart prayers become very personal conversations with God.

8

AN UNEXPECTED TURN

FOUR MONTHS AFTER Christian Experience Weekend, in June of 2011, we drove with our friends Bev and Dwight to Maryland. Seeing the beauty between Iowa and Maryland was incredible; I had always wanted to see the East and was not disappointed. We had arranged to stay at a timeshare in the Blue Ridge Mountains where we would enjoy a week of relaxing and golfing, which I was sincerely looking forward to.

My first day out on the course, I had trouble hitting the ball. I'm a pretty good golfer, so I didn't understand why my swing was so off—even Nancy, who admits to being a not-so-good golfer, was looking great compared to me. I chalked it up to golf's being a fickle game—and to being tired from working double duty the week prior to our trip—and tried to be good-natured as Nancy and our friends laughed and teased me without mercy each time I missed the ball or sliced it in the wrong direction.

Fortunately, golf was not our only focus. We also did some sightseeing in the mountains and took a quick trip to Washington D.C., which was a delight for Nancy and me as it was our first time there. We loved it all— Arlington, the monuments, the White House, the outdoor lunch on Pennsylvania Ave. We felt incredibly grateful to be able to enjoy it all and reveled in the fact that life was good.

Underneath my outward joy and gratitude, however, I felt tired and restless. I did my best to project that I was fine, but I really didn't feel like myself. I figured my overall malaise was related to the hives I had contracted back in December, when I had eaten some shrimp at a friend's house. That night, my lips started to swell, and by the next morning, my entire face was swollen, accompanied by an itchy rash. Nancy was worried that the stress I had taken on for the men's weekend was the cause, but I didn't agree; I believed it was just a short-lived reaction to the shellfish. But when the rash got worse and I couldn't bear the itching any longer, I finally went to a doctor. He prescribed a low dose of prednisone, which would relieve the symptoms while I was taking it, but as soon as the treatment was over, the rash would return. Eventually I was diagnosed with chronic hives, a condition I learned could be a problem forever—and evidenced by my continued sleep issues, overall fatigue, and recurring rash and swelling, I was inclined to believe that was true.

But the main reason we had made the trip to Maryland was to attend the U.S. Open in Bethesda, a true bucket-list item for me, and I wasn't going to let anything ruin it for me. We awoke that morning to the most beautiful day imaginable, and we arrived at the course to find breathless expanses of green and sunshine for what seemed miles on end—I was inclined to ask Nancy to pinch me, it was so dreamlike. It actually felt surreal that we were there.

We laid claim to four awesome seats in the bleachers by the sixth hole, surrounded by water, where we could see number seven's tee box and watch the pros head down the fairway in front of us. We were there for over six hours watching every twosome play through. I was in heaven watching the tournament, but sitting on the bleachers was difficult. I had spent many years on bleachers attending Matt's competitive swim meets, and I always struggled with it. This day was no different. I stood up and stretched numerous times, but it didn't do much good. There was no way I was missing any of the action, though, so I did my best to bear the pain.

After the last group had played through the sixth hole, everyone wanted to walk to see other holes. As Nancy rose, she glanced over at me and saw that I had my chin propped on my chest, looking down at the ground. She thought I was being silly until I told her that my neck and back hurt from sitting so long. She sat back down and elbowed me playfully. "Lee, put your head up!"

"I can't," I said.

"Seriously," she teased, "put your head up. You look like a goofball."

I struggled to tilt my chin toward her a little. "I can't," I said again.

"What?" she said, still thinking I was playing.

I then lifted my chin with my hands. "I can't hold up my head without supporting it."

Nancy saw the worry in my eyes, but we both blamed how long we'd been sitting on the bleachers and believed it would get better with time. So, not wanting to miss the opportunity, we went ahead to hole 18 and watched Rory McIlroy win the 2011 U.S. Open. It was a thrill to say the least, even though I had to hold my head up with my hands the entire time.

As we headed to the exit, Nancy suggested we stop at the medical tent for advice. All of the doctors had left by then, so the P.A. on duty gave me some Tylenol and a fresh bottle of water, encouraging me to get some rest. Since there was no other professional there to assess my condition, we left.

On the bus, Nancy began to massage my neck. We were sure I would get better after relaxing and maybe having a cocktail back at the condo. But by the next morning, I had lost complete control of the muscles in my neck, and the ensuing two-day drive back to Ankeny was filled with understandable angst and fear.

When we finally got home from our trip, a doctor at the clinic prescribed a muscle relaxer and sent me home. I wasn't convinced that would help—still anxious about having lost control of my muscles—but a couple of days later, I felt somewhat better. Nancy and her four girlfriends had their annual week in Florida together planned, and although Nancy was more than hesitant, I encouraged her to go.

Nancy's Journal
Beginning 1 July 2011

Each year for twenty years, I have been blessed with a "girls only" time. Five of us—Shelley, Jules, Kathy, Pert, and me, all wives, mothers, and teachers who love the sun and fun —convinced our husbands that this time away together was cheaper than a psychiatrist was. Wherever we gather, we're told that our never-ending chatter sounds like ducks quacking; hence we've been dubbed, "The Ducks." We plan a trip each year to fit everyone's schedules, and this year we determined that our trip would be the week after Lee and I went to Maryland. Lucky for me, packing is very easy for a Duck trip—a swimsuit, an outfit, sunglasses, a toothbrush, and a credit card is all I really need.

Although Lee is very self-sufficient, I was concerned about leaving him. He was not himself, but he appeared to be getting better. He promised to call me every day and report in. He also promised to see our family doctor, Denny. He insisted I go and that he would be fine, so I flew to Florida with the Ducks. We arrived on Sunday, June 26.

Lee held up his end of the bargain and called me every day, but I could tell he wasn't completely truthful with me. He said he felt a little better, but he hadn't played golf all week, which he brushed off by saying it would just take some time. I feared he was getting worse, not better, but he did get to see Dr. Denny. He and his wife, Sue, are very dear friends, and Sue has many connections in the medical arena. Dr. Denny was concerned and ordered an MRI for Friday, along with an appointment with a specialist. Dr. Denny wondered if the hives and the muscle problems were related.

Lee promised to call me after his 10:00 test was over on Friday, so I expected a call by noon. But noon came and went, and Lee hadn't called. I admit I got a little ticked off. I knew there would be no results, but he was supposed to call. So I phoned and left a not-so-friendly message. When he still didn't call, I left another message. No reply. Then, I texted a nasty message. Still no reply. Well ... Hmmm, I thought, that is just like a guy.

The second or third morning after Nancy's departure, I woke up at 6 a.m. gasping for air. My arms ached and I had a hard time moving. My first thought was, *I'm having a heart attack*, but rather than dial 911, I managed my way into some clothes, jumped into my pickup, and headed for the urgent care clinic five minutes away. It seemed like it would be faster than waiting for an ambulance.

After a couple of quick exams and X-rays, I was taken by ambulance to a Des Moines metro hospital. An EKG en route indicated my heart was fine, but I was still struggling for air, and the pain in my upper abdomen was excruciating. I could only speak one or two words before inhaling and speaking again, so it was a challenge to complete a sentence. I spent five hours in the emergency room with doctors trying to figure out the problem.

My cell phone was at home with all the phone numbers of family and friends; the only number I had memorized was Nancy's, and I decided not to call her in my condition. I didn't want to alarm her with my labored breathing, and I was sure it would pass. But as time went on, I gradually felt worse. Afraid I might not recover, I reluctantly borrowed a nurse's phone to call Nancy.

My mind froze as I listened to Lee's voice. It was weak, and it was obvious he was having trouble breathing. My finger was in my ear so I could hear him above the noise of the ocean waves: "Nanc, I'm in the hospital ... (Breath) ... having some trouble breathing ... (Gasping breath). I forgot my cell phone ... (Breath)... Can you give me Ken's number? ... (Breath) ... or call him to bring it?"... (Breath).

My mind was stuck. I wasn't breathing either. Lee was in the hospital gasping for air, and all I could think was: What the hell am I doing in Florida? What happened? How serious is this?

I turned to the Ducks and they knew by the look on my face that it was something awful. "Lee is in the hospital," I said. "He forgot his phone and can't breathe right." The atmosphere suddenly turned surreal. Phones were at their ears in seconds. Shelley, Jules, and Kath called their husbands. Pert scrambled to pick up beach gear. Jules stopped and said, "We need to call Sue. Lee needs Dr. Denny!" I hung up with Lee, assuring him we would get help to him ASAP.

Jules knows the ins and outs of air travel ... and so began many God moments. She did everything for me. All I had to do was hand her a credit card and answer some simple questions. Good thing—it was all I was capable of at that moment.

At the airport, I called the kids, attempting not to throw them into a panic. When I talked to Matt, I thought I sounded calm and reassuring, but his first words interrupted mine. "I feel I should hang up and be on the road to Des Moines."

I tried hard not to cry or sound as scared as I felt as I called Amy. She was not in Illinois, but in Iowa City (God-moment), making her only two hours from Des Moines *instead of the usual five and a half. Amy, after talking with Matt and Ken, called back to say she would be there on Saturday as Ken didn't think Lee was in imminent danger. But at some point Sue decided otherwise and urged the kids to come right away. They were already at the hospital when I arrived.*

After many prayers on both flights, held in God's hands the entire way, Ken and Sue picked me up at the airport at 10 p.m. They tried to prepare me for what I was going to face—that Lee was on oxygen, his muscles were shutting down, he could not hold his head up, and lifting his arms was difficult. They had already seen some very tense moments, and so had the kids.

When we arrived, God put a smile on my face, and a joke came out of my mouth. "You really wanted some attention, huh?" But I quickly realized that Lee was using all of his energy to breathe. Lying down was not an option as he couldn't breathe in that position and was barely breathing while sitting up. His eyes said, "I'm in big trouble here."

DOCTORS WERE GETTING NOWHERE, and getting there slowly. After most of the day in the ER, I was admitted to a room at 3 p.m. My lungs were collapsing, and three disappointing trips to the MRI station failed—each time I experienced severe pain when attempting to lie down. What's more, I stopped breathing.

They finally gave me a temporary breathing apparatus called a cannula, allowing me to take in more air, but it was hard work, uncomfortable, and extremely exhausting. Energy drained out of me as if I had a leak, and I truly wondered if that day would be my last. I was incredibly grateful to have my family and close friends with me, uncertain how much time I had left.

My condition baffled everyone. And to make matters worse, it was a long holiday weekend and doctors were in short supply. Being Friday, July 1, I had to wait until Tuesday, July 5 before seeing a specialist. Struggling for air for four days was the only option I had. Though it was hard to let her go that first night, Matt and I urged Nancy to go home and get some sleep.

The hours ticked by slowly as I sat in the chair with Amy by my side, praying I would recover, sleeping only a few hours. Then, on Saturday, a rheumatologist came to examine me. Nancy and Matt had returned by early morning, and I had a spark of hope until the doctor began speaking to me in a condescending tone, pushing on my muscles to test them while saying things like, "I could break you so easily" and "I'm a little guy and you're a big guy, but you're so weak." I could tell Nancy wanted to punch him; I was surprised Matt didn't.

He told us I needed a muscle test called an EMG, but that I couldn't have it done until Tuesday. I couldn't believe I would have to wait three whole days in the condition I was in; I honestly didn't think I would make it. But he coldly informed us that there was no such thing as an emergency EMG, no exceptions, then promptly left with no words of encouragement.

The next days were spent trying to make Lee as comfortable as possible. He transitioned from the cannula to a bi-pap, and although he was to use it only as needed, it was all the time at that point. We asked for a better recliner, since the bed was not working at all, but no others were available. Then our angel, Sue, called in some favors, and by July 4, Lee was moved to the "penthouse" of the hospital. He not only had a more comfortable reclining chair, the room was a suite with a couch, mini-kitchen, table and chairs, and even an extra guest bed.

Our family of four moved into this new space and spent the Fourth of July together, watching the fireworks set off at the ballpark over the Des Moines skyline. Afterward, Amy and I slept (sporadically) together in the guest bed while Matt dozed on the sofa. But Lee couldn't rest at all; he was becoming weaker and weaker. When a specialist came to do an ultrasound of his arm, he discovered Lee had developed a blood clot due to a bad IV. At that point, he needed blood thinners to prepare for the EMG the following day.

The evening of the fourth, I had also called Dwight at Lee's request. He wanted to be anointed, and Dwight could make these arrangements. Unbeknownst to me, Sister Susan had visited Lee at the hospital prior to my return from Florida, asking Lee about anointing. At the time, Lee had said that he wasn't that bad, but that had changed; he now felt ready. Fr. Steve, our parish pastor, was not available, so another friend, Fr. Greg, came and performed the Anointing of the Sick sacrament. It was a true blessing and gave Lee a grace he desperately needed, making him feel more calm and relieved. God had been made present to him.

The nurses had said that if he needed the bi-pap 24/7 he would have to be transferred to the ICU, and by Tuesday, that is exactly where we were. The move was traumatic because Lee needed to breathe through a portable bi-pap machine while being wheeled to the ICU, and he was terrified that he wouldn't be able to get enough air. It took lots of assurance to make the move, but the nurse, who was like a sweet, caring angel, was very kind and comforting. She had watched Lee quickly deteriorate in the penthouse, and he had made it through the last days because of her calm and perseverance.

In the ICU, the nurses were very restrictive at first, allowing only one person in the room at a time. No one was able to spend the night, and we felt we were being shut out. I was in a state of shock, but we dug in our heels—there was no way we were leaving him alone. We insisted as a family that one or all three of us would be staying the night. We agreed to limit visitors, but declared that Amy, Matt, and I would be in the room with him as much as we felt necessary. He had stopped breathing so many times already. We had to be there to make his frequent panic subside.

After reluctantly conceding to our terms, one nurse was kind enough to provide us with a marker board so that Lee could write to communicate. It was a wonderful distraction as we waited several hours for the EMG. Before that test could happen, however, Lee had to be intubated, which is a terrible thing for a conscious person to endure. I was shaking as they wheeled him away, knowing he would return with the breathing tube. If it hadn't been for my friends outside in the waiting area—my Ducks had returned from Florida to support me—I don't know how I would have gotten through it.

After the EMG was performed successfully, we were told that the muscle biopsy needed to be sent to Iowa City and that the results would take a week. We were stunned by this and felt certain Lee wouldn't last that long. I was ready to lose it when Matt quietly approached me and told me he had been in hourly phone contact with his friend Colleen, a neurologist at Kansas University Medical Center. She had already heard enough and thought Lee had the symptoms of an autoimmune neuromuscular disease.

Frustrated by the lack of communication between the neuro doctors and the muscular doctors who were on Lee's case—each had his own diagnosis and opinions, and they didn't seem to be communicating with each other—Matt sat me down with his sincere, compassionate manner.

"Mom, how would you feel about transferring Dad to KU Med Center?" he asked. "I've been talking to Colleen, and she thinks we need to get him there right away. They have the doctors, the expertise, and the facility to do what needs to be done. I know this won't be easy for you, being a long way from all of your support system, but I trust Colleen and she thinks it's what needs to happen."

I didn't hesitate long; I wanted Lee well, and I wanted him to live. Des Moines was trying but just didn't seem to be moving fast enough. I said, "Matt, I trust you on this. Let's do it!"

But wanting to do it and actually doing it were two very different things.

First, we had to have preauthorization from our insurance to transfer and be accepted at KU. Thankfully, Colleen was able to do the paperwork on that end, and Sue knew who to speak to in Des Moines, but it was a heated struggle for several hours nonetheless.

While Lee was getting weaker and more frustrated, we encountered various roadblocks. The insurance provider preferred that Lee stay in Des Moines; they would consider allowing him to transfer to Iowa City, but not Kansas City. With only one neuromuscular doctor in Iowa City and no specialized ICU, we refused to back down for the KU transfer. When they finally conceded, they declared insurance wouldn't pay for a helicopter; we would have to settle for land transfer by ambulance.

Though this was not ideal, we were relieved to get the green light. All we needed now was for a Des Moines doctor to sign a "medical letter of necessity." None of his doctors, however, were willing to do this; they still believed— whether from a place of hope or hubris—that they were capable of dealing with his situation. After another long struggle, a compassionate doctor finally stepped in and agreed to sign for Lee's release.

Many dear people helped us through what was, up till then, the most difficult time of our lives. Sue spent hours on the phone dealing with insurance issues; Shelley helped me pack for a long stay at a hospital three hours away from home. Dwight and Bev offered to drive my car to Kansas City so I would have transportation available. Matt was constantly on the phone with Colleen and his friends in KC preparing for our arrival, and Amy kept her dad semi-calm through each excruciating day. When he would get restless and have panic attacks, she was the only person who could talk him into slowing his breath, closing his eyes, and even sleeping. She became his best nurse ... and all who offered prayers for us became our angels.

9

TROUBLE

I T WAS VERY HOT, in the 90s it seemed. I had mixed
emotions—while incredibly grateful, I was frantic
about the transfer. Completely dependent on the
ventilator now, I was worried it would stop working and
fought the ICU nurse whose job it was to sedate me,
afraid I would never wake up. When she finally
succeeded, I was still uncomfortable. The heat was
stifling, so the two men in the ambulance placed ice
bags all over me before we left, which gave me a
modicum of relief.

It was comforting that Nancy was up front, but I
heard the EMT say to her, "Is your husband always this
anxious?"

"No," she said. "But wouldn't you be in his condition?"

The EMT softened a bit. "I'm really trying to keep him calm," he said. "He's doing better. We'll be there soon."

Every minute seemed to tick by, but they did their best to make the trip as comfortable as possible—and we did arrive faster than expected. Nancy's Beetle would make that trip in three hours and fifteen minutes. The ambulance got us there in two and a half hours.

WITHIN MY FIRST 24 HOURS in the KU Intensive Care Unit, I was diagnosed. As Colleen suspected on the phone through her conversations with Matt, I had an autoimmune disease called Myasthenia Gravis (MG).

Though I had believed my condition was related to the hives, I found out hives actually have nothing to do with MG, which typically advances very slowly over several years before reaching my stage. The disease usually begins with drooping of the eyelids to three-quarters closed. I, however, was not a usual case. In fact, my eyelids never drooped, even when doctors checked on a daily basis. For unexplained reasons, I went from Bethesda, Maryland, directly into crisis.

In simple terms, my muscles were methodically shutting down, starting at my neck and working downward. As I lost control over them, I lost control of my life. I couldn't breathe on my own, eat, talk, swallow, walk, or move my body without being moved by a nurse. My perfectly healthy mind became trapped in a non-functioning body. I kept hoping it was a bad dream, that the nightmare would end at any moment so I could go home, but as time went by, my hope diminished. I knew I had excellent care, but I couldn't help but fear that I was slowly dying—or worse, that I would live this way indefinitely.

One saving grace was that either Matt or Amy smuggled the dry-erase board from Des Moines. My handwriting declined rapidly, but I managed to scribble crude messages to my family with extreme effort and sloppy wrist motion. According to Nancy's journal, my first message was, "I won't let this get me."

KU MEDICAL CENTER IS a teaching hospital, so young doctors-to-be tagged along with MDs, and nurses-in-training accompanied certified nurses on just about every round of my care. For this reason, my intensive care unit was larger than normal to allow extra room for a posse. That room was my home for the next five weeks.

With floor-to-ceiling windows facing a control station, my room reflected ever-present nurses monitoring computerized vitals from the machines attached to me. My bed faced the glass wall; the opposite wall was all window, overlooking Kansas City and filling the room with sunlight.

Nancy was my constant protector, sleeping when she could in a reclining chair near my bed, and writing in her journal. Colleen was there that first night, along with an entourage of specialists, and she told Nancy it would be her job to write down the names and titles of all the doctors in the room, keeping track of everything they said and did on a daily basis. In doing so, this angel had given Nancy a purpose.

I quickly learned the unwritten law of hospital confinement: Sleep is not allowed. As all long-term patients do, I napped between intrusions. The solid wall in my room had cupboards and counters, and all were peppered with cards of well wishes and prayers. When poked and prodded during sleep interruptions, peering at the cards gave me strength.

During the day, and many times in the middle of the night, Nancy would read to me from the 17,000-plus posts on Caring Bridge, a hospital media website service designed for communication between patient, friends, and family. The prayers and kind words of encouragement were overwhelming, and they made my bouts of sleeplessness almost welcome.

Since I had developed a blood clot in my left arm in Des Moines, I was down to one arm for the never-ending needle pokes. Compounding things further, I was diagnosed with pneumonia in my right lung on July 11. The left lower lung was still collapsed, confirming I had myositis, or inflammation of the skeletal muscles. Most Myasthenia Gravis patients do not have this condition, and because I had both, massive doses of steroids followed—500mg twice a day. In addition, I would receive a total of nine plasmapheresis treatments over the next weeks, which exchange plasma cells to remove antibodies in treating autoimmune conditions.

By July 15, I received another blow: a biopsy report showed I had a thymoma, which was actually good news compared to the alternative suspect—lymphoma. A thymoma meant the thymus gland was abnormally enlarged and a tumor was growing, so a decision was made to remove the thymus by opening my chest wall. Ninety-eight percent of the tumor was removed during the surgery, and later in my recovery, I would receive thirty radiation treatments to destroy the remaining two percent.

The next days were long and blurred with the coming and going of doctors and nurses, Nancy's ever-present love, and what seemed to be non-ending tests and assessments. Then, on July 21, I was told that they would remove my breathing tube the next day. On one hand, I was elated, yet I lay wide awake at midnight worried, anticipating the procedure. For the past three weeks, I had become dependent on this tether and couldn't get calm or comfortable. But twenty-two days on a ventilator reached beyond the limits of my doctor's preference, so I had no choice but to find out if I could once again breathe on my own.

10

BREATHE

ON FRIDAY, JULY 22, 2011, Nancy posted a plea for prayers that I accept the biggest challenge so far. No one knew if I would be able to breathe with my damaged and weak lungs or if my diaphragm muscles would work again, and my own anxiety mounted.

A team of doctors, interns, and nurses surrounded my bed as I scribbled on the marker board, asking if it would be okay to wear Nancy's earphones during the procedure. I was relieved when they said it wouldn't be a problem, and I listened to the "Divine Mercy Chaplet" as the specialists proceeded. It calmed my nerves and gave me some peace.

My split breastbone from the thymectomy surgery was sewn together with titanium wire, and my chest wound was stapled, giving me pain and much distress as the tubes were pulled. I could not breathe in or out. My body was facing the specialists and I couldn't turn my head to see Nancy, who was just out of sight to my right. My eyes were pleading with the specialists for air as I knew I couldn't hold on much longer. I wanted to see Nancy. More than anything, I wanted to hold her in my arms just one more time to tell her I loved her. Somehow, I touched the marker board with my hand and someone instantly handed me the marker. With no time left, I couldn't tilt the board up to see it, so I quickly scrawled, "love you see you in heaven." Nancy knew the message was for her, but out of the corner of my eye, I saw her hand come to the board and wipe it clean as if to tell me, "You are not leaving me."

Then everything went dark.

11

MIRACLE OF MIRACLES

I WAS FLOATING IN A place that was pure black, a hundred times more black than I have ever seen. There were no walls or floors; I could not see my body because I had no body. I was simply there. I wasn't struggling to breathe because I didn't need to breathe. I seemed to be vertical with no aches or pains.

Time was standing still. I could hear the "Divine Mercy Chaplet" playing in crystal clear stereo, clearer than ever before. But nothing was happening, so I spoke through my thoughts.

God, am I dying? Am I dead? What is this place? Why am I here? Why is this taking so long? This is not the way I thought I would die.

Nothing.

Is God deciding what to do with me? I wondered.

Anxious and humble, I prayed through my thoughts. *If this is Your will, I totally and completely surrender. I have been anointed. I am ready.*

Immediately after expressing this thought, I heard the sound of thunder. As it cracked, I felt something akin to acid burning inside my chest. Light began to shine down from above, and though it seemed as though my head didn't actually exist, I looked up and saw brilliance coming from far above, as through glitter or sparkly snowflakes. After a few seconds (in earth time), they began to drift and flutter downward in slow motion toward me. In tiny shards of a clear glass-like substance, the sparkles floated down and began to swirl slowly into a giant vortex, like water spiraling down a drain. The closer they fell toward me, the faster the vortex spun, until I could see the amazing colors of the sparkles.

The whirlpool of crystals turned faster as they came closer to my head, but out in front of me. They moved so rapidly that they appeared like multicolored dashes, elongated sparkles all culminating in a point at the bottom. When the dashes were just above me, I heard the sound of hundreds and hundreds of people talking, all at the same time. I floated closer, leaning into the vortex to listen. The sounds were the voices of people praying, all different prayers, each in different parts of a prayer. Every dash was a prayer spoken by an individual

—voices of men, women, and children. I literally *saw,* and then *heard,* and then *felt* each prayer as it flew past. These were the voices of my family, friends, church community, and strangers. These were my prayer warriors.

12

JESUS

FLOATING BACKWARD AWAY FROM the vortex, I could see the dashes flowing in a downward spiral, picking up speed and more light as they gathered toward the bottom. The colored dashes compressed into a bright light like a welder's arc, as if I was looking into the sun. As the last dashes converged, the light burst, and I was staring into the face of Jesus Christ, only inches away.

Shocked, I backed up. In contrast to the deep, black abyss, brilliant gold, white, and yellow rays radiated outward from within Him, somewhat blurring my vision of Him. It was as if He was illuminated from within. Other warm colors I have never seen before radiated from Him as well.

I used to think of halos as hollow circles depicted behind or above the heads of angels, saints, and holy people in paintings. Jesus' halo, however, was in 4D, jutting out in every direction. No artist could paint this halo, and I was transfixed by it, in complete awe. It seemed like I gazed for hours, speechless. Jesus' brown wavy hair came down to His shoulders, and His short brown beard had soft waves. I looked for scars but saw none because His hair covered His forehead. His nose was what I would call "Roman," and He was handsome in every sense of the word.

Then my eyes locked on His and I could look nowhere else. They were all colors in one, but mostly dark blue, and what struck me most intensely was how kind, gentle, and mesmerizing they were. When I looked into those eyes, I couldn't see the rest of His body.

No words were spoken, but His thoughts invaded mine. I internalized words of His love for me ... impressions of prayer ... thoughts of my free will and God's will ... feelings of trust ... and, ultimately, feelings of hope.

13

MOTIVATION

I N AN INSTANT, I was jolted back into my bed in the ICU. All my old feelings of nausea, pain, and weakness returned. I found myself tethered to the same life-saving equipment as before, smelling the familiar odors of the hospital. The sounds of my machines and people talking filled the room. The ventilator was in place, reinstalled and supplying the oxygen I desperately needed.

The entire near-death experience took place in less than two minutes, but it seemed like I had been away for hours. When it ended in a flash, it was like being shaken from the most perfect and wonderful dream. I wanted to go back. I *really* wanted to go back.

Though I was bursting inside with intense feelings of joy, I realized I couldn't share the experience with anyone until the moment was right. I would like to say I needed more time to comprehend the enormity of the experience, that I was not physically strong enough to announce this miracle of miracles. But the truth was, I was afraid. I therefore tucked it into the vault temporarily, where not even Nancy could know.

The best way I can describe the experience is that it was supernatural medicine that gave me the motivation to overcome my illness. I began to gain strength and have spurts of energy. I felt an urgent need to get back home to Iowa so I could give the message from Jesus to everyone, especially my prayer warriors. It didn't matter what people would think of me; I was given a message for anyone who would listen. I believed with all my heart that Jesus wanted me to do this, and I became obsessed with becoming His disciple.

MY FIRST GOAL WAS to get out of that bed, but complications and frequent setbacks slowed down my recovery, and at times I even regressed. But my friends, family, and spirituality held me up and kept me energized. I refused to give up, and over time, with dogged persistence, I relearned how to move my muscles, walk, talk, and even breathe. The human body is a magnificent creation, complex beyond anyone's understanding, and I watched it miraculously repair itself. Although I know it may sound strange, I sometimes feel God blessed me with Myasthenia Gravis, precisely so that I would appreciate His creation more. And I do. I sincerely came to believe that my temporary loss was also my gain.

At some point, I transitioned from the ventilator to a tracheostomy tube, a breathing tube placed surgically in my throat. Then, several days later, I was finally able to breathe on my own again, without the trach. Once it was removed, relearning to swallow was a scary ordeal and proved to be the most difficult step of my recovery. I feared that I would choke or aspirate food into my lungs, so it took quite a while before I mastered it. But my overall determination paid off. After five weeks in ICU, and one week in acute rehab, I was released from the hospital.

My muscles, especially in my upper body, were still weak, and I was given strict instructions to pace myself and listen to my body to avoid another crisis, but I was home. The agenda was to rest for a few days, look at several rehab options, and meet with the radiation oncologist. I also required more outpatient physical, occupational, and speech therapy. Swallowing soft food was still very difficult, and my stomach feeding tube was kept in place in case swallowing totally failed.

Despite all of that, however, it was Christmas in August. What a homecoming I received! The entire neighborhood greeted us with signs in their yards, and the Ducks had cleaned the house spotless. Nancy was determined that I follow the doctor's orders by not overdoing it, maintaining the title she had earned in the hospital of "Nazi Nancy"—no hostile references intended—for having had to restrict my visitors. In fact, some of our neighbors' yard signs lightheartedly read: "Welcome home Lee and Nazi Nancy."

Though I was overjoyed to be home again, my ability to walk was limited. Over the course of the next four months, I gradually regained strength and improved, in spite of a few setbacks along the way. I began physical therapy sessions in September, which were a wonderful boost to my muscle strength but by late September, I was experiencing severe back pain. Massive doses of steroids had taken their toll, and I had developed "drug-induced osteoporosis." I had shrunk from 5'11" to 5'8" as a result of serious spine curving, and my brittle vertebrae would fracture at the slightest lean forward. To protect me from future breaks, I was fitted with an aluminum brace to keep me upright at all times.

Another side effect of the steroids was ballooning to 40 pounds heavier. My self-esteem dropped because of it, but Nancy reminded me that I was on the road to a healthier me, so I offered my pain up to God in exchange for His grace. By placing my faith totally in Him, I gained strength and overcame much of my adversity. I prayed often for Mary's intersession, and each prayer built a stronger relationship with God and Mary. As a result, more grace followed.

Recovery involved seemingly countless meetings

with rehab physicians in both Kansas and Iowa. Upon reviewing my medical history, several doctors repeated the exact same words, "You have been to hell and back." Upon hearing this, I would always smile and say nothing. Inside, I said to myself, "I was closer to *heaven* and back." Physical therapists were amazed at my progress. They called me the miracle man. If they only knew ...

Myasthenia Gravis still had a grip on me, but I didn't want it getting in the way of fulfilling my next goal, one that Nancy wasn't aware of: to personally thank the prayer warriors who helped get me home. In addition to that, I felt compelled to give them the message from Jesus, which Nancy still did not know either. Before this could happen, however, I needed to finally share it with her. I was sincerely ready to burst from containing this holiest of holy time of my life.

One evening, my Knights of Columbus insurance agent visited our home. Nancy and I were sitting around our kitchen table reviewing policies when my agent, Matt, said something that triggered a response from me, unwittingly spilling part of my secret. Nancy's and Matt's eyes began to water as I continued to expound, clearly surprised by what I had experienced. Although I didn't go into deep detail at the time, as I wanted to save the specifics for Nancy alone before sharing with others, both were visibly moved.

Needless to say, this set the mood for sharing the entire experience with Nancy, and after Matt left, I opened my vault once again and released every facet of the incredible incident that had happened to me during that fateful day in the hospital. The feeling was euphoria as Nancy took my hands from across the table and tears flowed from each of us. As she took it all in with her characteristic loving way, Nancy now understood precisely why I had been so adamant about speaking to our prayer warriors ... and she set out to find a way to make it happen.

CHRISTMAS CAME AGAIN IN SEPTEMBER—the 25th to be exact—when I finally received my opportunity to share my experience with my prayer warriors at an open house "Thank You" evening at Our Lady's Immaculate Heart Church.

I entered the room to a full house of dear friends, who applauded me as I made my way down the front, greeting and gently hugging people. Then I slowly ascended the stage to retrieve my notes from the podium, telling the crowd to forgive my nervousness and lack of public speaking skills, as I found my place in the middle of the stage. Though many eyes were on me, I believed I had been called to do this and that the Holy Spirit was with me, putting the words in my mouth. In fact, I never needed my notes at all.

I knew the guests were concerned about my health, as it had only been a month since I was discharged from the hospital, so I began by giving them an update on my condition. I then shared about the miracles I had witnessed, one by one over my lifetime, culminating with my near-death experience ... and the message that was so profoundly given to me to share.

Jesus had spoken to me without words, and I felt like a child as I looked into His eyes and absorbed His message. It will live forever, embedded into every fiber of my being:

*He so dearly and deeply loves us as if each one
of us is His only child.
Our prayers truly matter to God.
Each and every one of our prayers is always
heard by Him.
Remember that our will is not God's will.
Our plan is not His plan.
There is a purpose for everything in God's plan.
Respect His plan.
Trust Him.
In trust, we will receive Hope and Peace.*

AFTER RECEIVING THE GIFT of sharing God's message with my prayer warriors, I was filled with an inexplicable joy. And although I continued to struggle with stamina, fatigue, and vertebrae issues, another ray of sunshine entered my life—in the form of a once-in-a-lifetime opportunity.

In late October 2011, I was asked by the Diocese of Des Moines to design and construct a Holy Water Font for their upcoming 100th Year Anniversary Celebration to be held at HyVee Hall in downtown Des Moines. The Sunday event, scheduled for November 6, was only a few days away, but my design juices immediately began to flow again as I took up the challenge—albeit with a bit of anxiety.

I had spent my entire career outdoors, in contact with nature, bending and squatting and surveying the landscape from every angle to arrive at the perfect design. This time, however, I would have to assess the project sitting in a wheelchair.

Despite what could have been a setback, the design was in my head even before seeing the site conditions. With only six hours to construct my vision of a font on a concrete floor, I called into play my rank as a Fourth Degree Knight of Columbus and solicited the services of our Assembly to perform the construction. Not only did they graciously agree, but my vendors stepped forward to offer free materials.

Over the next few days, God worked more magic as my team and I built what felt like another miraculous gift, all with no cost for materials or labor due to each person's extreme generosity. The enthusiasm was so high for the project that we all seemed fueled by that alone, working without reservation. We truly felt like humble servants of God.

By the time the event arrived, a beautiful baptismal font welcomed visitors into the hall. They were greeted by a 10' x 10' elevated pool containing three ancient Greek columns, each one a fountain with slow-running water flowing out of the top and splashing into the pool, and sitting atop each column were clear glass vessels of holy oils. The pool was embellished with living, colorful flowers and lighting, while stairs went up into the pool at one corner and out on the other side, symbolizing the entrance for a baptism. As guests poured in, children quickly gathered on the stairs, dipping their hands into the water as adults blessed themselves with the holy water. Everyone appeared taken by the creation, and I was again filled with joy.

ONE OF THE GREATEST pleasures in my profession had always been seeing the clients interacting with the end product. Whether the experience encompassed a simple stroll up a new, landscaped walkway bordered with hedges and flowers, or a tour of awe through an elaborate garden, or the realization of vision the client had only seen thus far on paper that was received with pure elation, those moments made every ounce of work worthwhile. Now, with this latest creation being the first since I became ill, I entertained hope that my company would no longer have to be on standby, and I embraced my renewed love for design with boosted morale and energy.

14

GOD IS IN THE DETAILS

TODAY, IN THE AUTUMN of my life, I am a retired landscape architect. The continued effects of my disease cause fatigue and I can no longer give 100% to my efforts. After harvesting over forty wonderful years in the business, I can't help but look back with incredible pride in the career that allowed me to embrace my passion. Not only did I love the creativity and communion with nature, but I found a way to incorporate God into my work. It took me almost half my career to hone this achievement, but once I did, it became part of everything I did.

My designs were a form of art, and my art was a form of loving God. During my studies at ISU, I was fascinated to learn that many artists place secret messages or hidden meaning into their paintings, known only to themselves or a select few. Yes, I am an artist— perhaps of a different sort—but I was no less inspired to use this technique. My canvas was the earth, and I hid Biblical meaning in each landscape design I produced. My impressions, however, remained between God and me; I never shared this secret homage with clients. It was a personal form of prayer and had meaning only to my Heavenly Father and me.

In order for you to fully envision the tributes I made to God in my work, I will open my vault one last time to share a few secrets ...

AN EARLY CLIENT HAD requested that I plant a shade tree in his front yard. After doing so, I placed a small rock under it without mentioning the meaning to the client. I was thinking of the verse where Jesus said to Peter (paraphrasing): "You are my rock, and upon this rock I shall build my church." After laying down the rock as a symbol, I asked that St. Peter watch over the family who lived in the house and show them God's church, in whatever way it would make sense to them.

ANOTHER CLIENT LIVED IN a rural home with a large family. The property had substantial acreage that was begging for landscape help, and my pre-design interview revealed that there were serious family-related problems within the home. I instinctively knew it wasn't my place to insert myself directly into their affairs, so I instead held the family up in prayer through my art. I created a Noah's Ark design, which I believed would be a safe haven for the family. I incorporated sweeping waves of changing plant heights to represent the choppy waters through which the family was traveling, and I chose pleasant pastel colors to make the home calm and soothing. Finally, I added a few upright evergreens to reflect their Guardian Angels. While the family had no idea I had built prayers for them right into their land, it made me happy to know I had left something heartfelt behind for them in hopes of inviting happier tomorrows.

IN 2001, I WAS honored to design the landscape plan for the building and ten acres of grounds at Our Lady's Immaculate Heart Catholic Church (OLIH) in Ankeny, the home parish where Nancy and I have been members for over 40 years, raised our children, and received many sacraments.

In one area of this design, I was inspired to hide a triangle of three identical Coralburst Flowering Crabapple trees, located directly south of the worship space. As I'm sure you can imagine, the trees represented the Holy Trinity: the Father, the Son, and the Holy Spirit. Ironically—and quite unexpectedly—one of the three trees died. Since only God and I knew the meaning of the trees, I couldn't help but wonder if He had a hand in the tree's death. I purposely did not replace it until the next planting season, selfishly and privately grieving the loss of the Son.

In another area, along the east wall of the worship space, I planted a lone Weeping Jade Flowering Crabapple to symbolize Mary Magdalene, the repentant prostitute who loved Jesus and wept as He carried the cross to His crucifixion. On the north wall, I placed a pair of Spring Snow Flowering Crabapples to represent Mary and Joseph. These trees are sterile and don't produce fruit—I knew it was a stretch of artistic license, but my reasoning was that Mary and Joseph did not produce their child through the usual means.

As you may conjecture, many more secrets are planted at Our Lady's Immaculate Heart ...

MY LIST GOES ON to cover a stretch of many years of taking God to work with me, and I utilized several techniques to pray at work. Some Biblical secrets were designed into the landscape via a symbolic plant name, such as the perennial "Obedient Plant," or the climbing rose called "Stairway to Heaven." Some secrets were hidden by plant character, like *weeping* or *sterile* as described above. Still others were concealed by assigning a saint to a particular plant, such as St. Francis to any tree in the design if the client had a pet. Sometimes I used specific features to strengthen a client's weakness —such as water as a reminder of baptism, or statuary for particular symbolism—while other times I let the design tell the prayer for me, or rather a prayer unfolded before my eyes as the result of my technical, architectural, or design elements coming together.

Most of the time, my plans included rose plants, which were symbolic of receiving the affection of the Blessed Virgin Mary, and I planted pyramidal evergreen trees—dominant plants that grow tall and strong—as guardian angels to protect a fragile client.

Regardless of how I got there, though, the most rewarding part of offering these private prayers was that they went unnoticed, except by God and me. Today, when I drive past local, matured projects and recall my prayers at a glance, I can't help but wonder if they made a difference. I certainly hope so.

15

THE FRUITS OF THE SPIRIT

TO THIS DAY, every morning when I wake, I joyfully relive every second of the memory of my near-death experience before rising. At night, I go to bed thanking God for another day with Him in my life. That experience will never leave me, and I can say, without reservation, that I am no longer afraid to die. My heart skips a beat when I think about what is waiting for you and me.

Miracles happen every day. I am positive you have witnessed a few at some time in your life, even if you didn't see them as such. Maybe they were not life-altering miracles, but obvious ones surround us everywhere. Look at a flower, or a tree, or into the eyes of a newborn, or your loved ones, or even your friends, especially when they smile or cry. You are looking into the eyes of God. He is among us.

As I expressed earlier, I am more than eager to get to heaven, but I also realize that I'm still preparing. God obviously has plans for me before I go, and until then, I will continue to share my spirituality with whomever will listen. Winter is just around the corner for me, and whatever days I have left belong to Him.

Like a squirrel gathering food to store for winter sustenance, I believe we should be gathering God's fruits, starting right now, no matter where we are in life's journey. The first step is always a prayer—a simple prayer can open hearts and will allow God to enter, even if only for a glimpse. He already knows what we are thinking, but He wants to *hear* our prayers from our lips. I don't believe there is any prayer God wouldn't listen to with compassion, any confession of secrets stowed away that he wouldn't understand. Whatever wrongs we may have committed, there is always space for repentance and forgiveness. Remember, you are His child.

I, myself, for one example, made a mistake early in my landscaping career for which I've had to ask for forgiveness—both from God and from my family. For the first twenty years in my profession, my goal was to use my talents, abilities, and God-given gifts to make a comfortable living for my family and me. I accomplished this goal; however, the false fruits of working long hours for financial gain came with a cost. I missed many important days with Nancy, Matt, and Amy that I cannot get back. It's great to have financial success and to own a nice home and expensive things, but they are only that: *things*. I wish I could go back to create the balance between work and family that I achieved after those first twenty years of work. It's possible to manage both work and family, with a high level of financial success, as long as there is balance.

What I've discovered is that the *real* fruit comes when I use my gifts to help others, especially the poor. Years ago, I joined a men's fraternity called the Knights of Columbus, which to me is the epitome of discipleship. We raise money to support hundreds of good causes, not only locally, but also internationally. I'm the guy who proudly hands out Tootsie Rolls at the grocery store, wearing a bright yellow and red apron. The end game is to provide financial help to the mentally handicapped. I believe in the Knights so strongly that I handed out Tootsie Rolls while in a wheelchair with fractured vertebra, and I know my fellow Knights in Wisconsin will do the same for my brother Steve. You, too, can experience this kind of joy simply by joining any group that promotes helping others. Discover how good it makes you feel working with God.

To quote Catholic Cardinal Francis Arinze:

If you have clothes in your closet you have not worn in two years, they don't belong to you. They belong to the poor. If you have shoes that have not been worn for two years, they do not belong to you. They belong to the poor.

God has provided all of us with talents, abilities, and special gifts to be used for a purpose, and that purpose is *not* solely for financial gain. There is nothing wrong with having financial abundance, but when we do, we should think of those who have less and give what we can. Our true purpose is to harvest the "Fruits of the Spirit"—which reminds me of a song by Points of Grace called "How You Live (Turn Up the Music)." If I may paraphrase a few words:

> Don't spend your life looking back,
> it's not who you knew,
> it's not what you did,
> it's how you lived.

If you're able, I encourage you to seek out this song and listen carefully to the words. I feel certain you'll find it inspiring.

I STRIVE TO KEEP my spirituality alive. It has become a way of life for me. I try not to turn it on and off like a light switch only when needed, but rather to live my actions through example, careful to avoid vanity or recognition. I often think of a refrigerator magnet I see at my friend's house that reads, "You can preach a better sermon with your life than with your lips."

I hope that is what I will continue to do.

EPILOGUE

WHEN GOD CHOSE ME to be His messenger, I had a hard time reconciling it. I didn't feel special enough; after all, I am no different from you, perhaps with the exception of a particularly heavy vault. When I had my near-death experience, I was inspired to take a long, hard look into my past to answer why He thought me worthy. Many recollections had been locked up for years, but when I sought to relive those life experiences, the dark secrets were no longer there. They had vanished because I faced those demons head on, leaving only the three miracles—Grandma, CEW, and Jesus—shining like a light.

Concentrating on those remarkably memorable events, it struck me: the milestone steps in my life were

God's secret homages to me, much like my secret prayers hidden in landscape designs were my homages to Him. I realized that my life on earth at this time and place is God's complex work of art, and that it contains intense significance to those around me. The miracles I experienced were all connected, and I saw my path, woven together with a simple common thread ... *prayer.*

But I understood that it wasn't only prayer in itself that laid the stones to my path; it was my *fervent* prayer. When I had prayed and witnessed my grandma's miracle, the Christian Experience Weekend miracle, the landscape design symbols, and Dad's funeral prayer, I had done so with *emotion,* and *reverence,* and *passion.* Then, in my last extraordinary miracle, Jesus showed me how my family, friends, neighbors, relatives, church community, and strangers prayed with that same emotion, reverence, and passion—for me. Afterward, God spared me to share His message with you. I truly believe that this is why God placed me on earth at this time and place.

We Christians are gracious people of prayer. I used to think some prayers were not heard or answered, but Jesus showed me they were all heard. Always. Many were answered the way I had hoped, and many have not been answered—yet. Sometimes, when I prayed in the past, the answers were not what I asked for. Now I know why: It is His plan we are living, not ours.

God knows that sometimes we are in great pain and suffering. As difficult as it may be, we must find a way to trust and respect God's will, continuing to pray and never giving up on prayer, whether answered as hoped or answered in a way we have yet to understand.

As for my near-death experience, I witnessed firsthand that God truly exists.

John 3: 16

God so loved the world that He gave His only begotten Son so that whoever believes in Him shall not perish, but will have eternal life.

Winter is just around the corner. I will be praying for you.

AUTHOR'S NOTE

Within six months after being discharged from the hospital, I was using a putter at the golf course. Over the next two years, I graduated to chipping, then to fairway woods, and finally to using a driver. My game will never be what it was, but some of my friends joke it never was that good! I have learned to read my body and take many breaks to avoid my archenemy—fatigue —but the fact that I'm here at all and living life is truly a miracle.

As for being charged with delivering the message of God's love for us ...

A friend recorded a video of my "Thank You" open house event so I could send it to my friends and family in Wisconsin. If you would like to view my nervous attempt to share some of my story and deliver the message, I humbly invite you to visit:

http://vimeo.com/30707333

ACKNOWLEDGMENTS

To my precious prayer community, I can only thank you with good deeds. As a humble layman, I will greet you at the door. I will seat you in your pew. I will pass the basket for your donations to the poor. I will minister the Holy Eucharist. I will place ashes on your forehead. I will prepare your Lenten meal. I will wash your feet. I will visit when you are sick. I will keep you in my prayers.

To my soul mate, Nancy, and my adult children, Matthew and Amy, for standing vigil over me during my darkest hours in ICU, thank you for being who you are —a loving and caring family.

A special thank you goes to the caretakers at Kansas University Medical Center. Your expertise, loving care, and concern for my health does not go unnoticed.

I could not have written this book without the amazing help of my editor and partner, Stacey Aaronson. Aside from being a supreme editor, her attention to so many details challenged me to dig deeper into my vault for more information than I was originally willing to give.

Most of all, I wish to express my gratitude to God Almighty for giving me the courage to tell this story and to be His disciple.

LEE BREITKREUTZ spent nearly forty years as a landscape architect, where he built personal homages to God into every design. After being diagnosed with a grave autoimmune disease in 2011, he was forced to semi-retire, but he continues to live his passion of designing beautiful landscapes, mostly for charity. He treasures the miracles he witnessed during his life that changed his spiritual perspective, and he is grateful to be alive.

Lee resides in Ankeny, Iowa, with his beloved wife, Nancy, where they are active members of Our Lady's Immaculate Heart Catholic Church. They are the proud parents of Matthew and Amy and will be first-time grandparents in October, 2014.

CPSIA information can be obtained at www.ICGtesting.com
Printed in the USA
LVOW12s2011100914

403482LV00002B/8/P